THE BRIDGE OF SIGHS

The Miami University Press Poetry Series
General Editor: James Reiss

THE BRIDGE OF SIGHS

Poems by
Steve Orlen

Miami University Press

Library of Congress Cataloging-in-Publication Data

Orlen, Steve, 1942–
    The Bridge of Sighs : poems / by Steve Orlen.
        p. cm. — (The Miami University poetry series)
    ISBN 1–881163–00–8. — ISBN 1–881163–01–6 (paper)
    I. Title.   II. Series.
PS3565.R577B7 1992
811'.54—dc20   92–8418
                                                    CIP

Text and jacket design by Sara Udstuen.
Printed by Malloy Lithographing, Ann Arbor, MI.

The paper in this book meets the guidelines
for permanence and durability of the Committee
on Production Guidelines for Book Longevity
of the Council on Library Resources. ∞

Printed in the U.S.A.

9 8 7 6 5 4 3 2 1

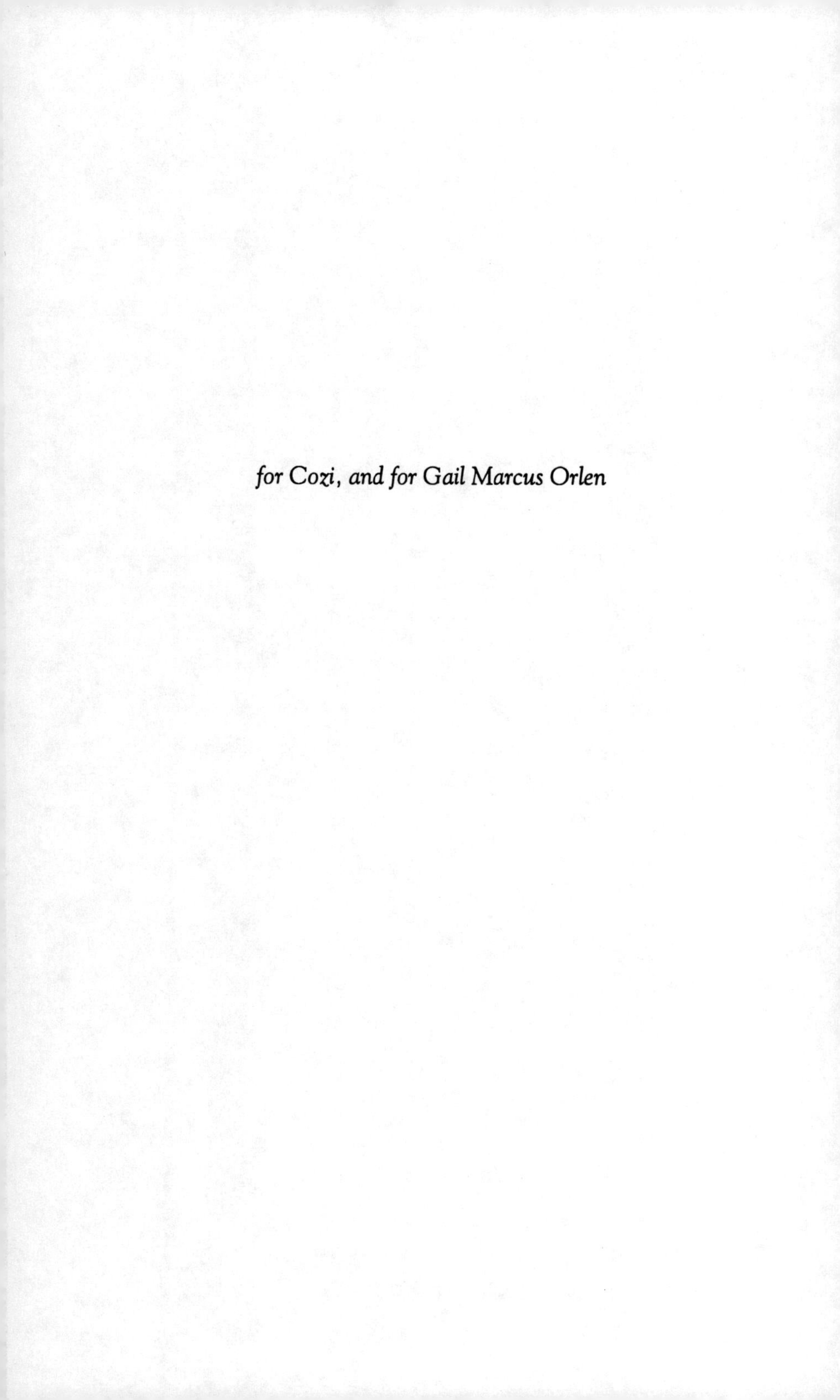

for Cozi, and for Gail Marcus Orlen

Also by Steve Orlen

Sleeping on Doors
Separate Creatures
Permission to Speak
A Place at the Table

Contents

III. *ELEGY*

ACKNOWLEDGMENTS

The American Poetry Review: Short Story, Carmen

Antaeus: Paradise

The Atlantic: The Bridge of Sighs

Columbia: A Magazine of Poetry & Prose: Conversation with the Dead

Crazyhorse: Acts of Will, Alternate Lives

High Plains Literary Review: Acrobatics

Ironwood: Red Leaves

New England Review: Religious Feeling, Acts of God, A Family of Three

Poetry: Celebrity, Shame

Poetry East: Standing in Line for *The Pickle Family Circus,* Child Care, The Big Difference

Raccoon: Porch Life

Seneca Review: At the Indoor Shopping Mall, Snapshots from An Album

Sonora Review: Familiar

The Best American Poetry 1989 (edited by Donald Hall and David Lehman, Scribners, 1989): The Bridge of Sighs

The Bread Loaf Anthology of Contemporary American Poetry (edited by Robert Pack, Sydney Lea, and Jay Parini, University Press of New England, 1985): Life Drawing, A House

The Morrow Anthology of Younger American Poets (edited by Dave Smith and David Bottoms, William Morrow and Company, 1985): Life Drawing

The New American Poets of the '80's (edited by Jack Myers and Roger Weingarten, Wampeter Press/Poetry International, 1984): Acts of Grace (under title, Acts Without Consequence), A House, Paradise

I would like to thank the National Endowment for the Arts, and the Arizona Council on the Arts for their support. And Centrum, and Fondation Karolyi of Vence, France, for residencies.

Thanks also to Tony Hoagland, Jon Anderson, and Richard Cummins for their editorial help.

For a brief moment Shepherd felt that emotion,
the opposite of déjà vu: not that he had been
there before but that he would never be there again.

Laguna Heat, T. Jefferson Parker

I
Snapshots from an Album

You can almost see
Who we were back then
Before the story begins: snow
On the trees, a house,
Some stars, or what would
Have been stars
If it weren't for the snow,
The falling, million,
Independent flakes
Simplifying some evergreens,
Shaping, being shaped
In endless argument. . . .

A FAMILY OF THREE

Supper done, and dishes, the bath,
Pajamas and the evening glass

Of milk. Light in all the rooms is waning
From the pruned-back habits

Of the day's stories. We sit
Before the picture window watching

The last light leave
The backyard, darkening the clothesline,

The garden hose, and a wishbone
Of patio chairs, and one blue

Skeletal palo verde tree
With eked-out golden blooms.

And flocks of various birds rush down
From a cloudless sky

In muddled grays and browns,
All looking too much alike

To call them beautiful
Or name them from *The Book*

Of Birds open on the coffee table.
They line up at the house-like,

Opaque plastic window feeder
In a fast thrashing

Of wings and knuckled beaks,
Scrambling for seed.

We watch this every evening through glass,
Three of them, three of us,

Until the dark takes them
Away from us and us from them.

ORDER

The boy wakes in his crib, picks up one toy
After another, examining, discarding,
Making those throaty clicks, naming out loud—
Guy   ball   elf   book—putting some on his right,
Some on his left, some behind, just out of sight.
Others he tosses from his crib. They make soft
Thuds on the rug, counting, accounting,
First in darkness, then delight, already a hoarder
And a judge. *Yes!* the toys are in order.
The morning may commence. *Yes! yes!*
He yells, then calls for his morning juice.

CHILD CARE

He doesn't want to go there but he goes
Into the mouth of the monster — in this case,
This morning, the new mother-sort-of-person
Who welcomes him at the door in that overly-accustomed,
Hearty, necessarily false way of all-day mothers
To the children of strangers. This is the life, kid.
Every place you go it's the same shabby, overused,
Slightly greasy teddy bear, and the TV tuned
To the same cartoon characters banging away at each other,
And different faces with similar names eyeing the new kid
With his thumb stuck in his mouth. Oh, they've almost
Got your number already, they've got their tongues
Hanging out. Isn't it convenient how the world
Lays itself out into such predictable types?
The biter, and the whiner, and the gentle soul,
The pouter you can bend to your will — if only
You knew which one was which. It won't take long, individual
Mouse of mine, clinging to my thigh, to discover
What really matters: who's quick or slow to anger,
Which is the tightest corner to defend.

Standing in Line for *The Pickle Family Circus*

You can tell it is bursting out of her, some accusatory snarl,
Something to upset the children, out of the teenage
Retarded girl in our midst as we stand in a raggedy line
For the small circus in a small-town ball park by the sea
Among the gulls who vie for the stray popcorn.
She paces among us, threading our line,
Tugging herself this way and that like a bulldog
On a leash so my son clings tighter to my leg, demanding
"Papa, hold me!" All the parents here
Are thinking we would like to hide her in a hole, and how lucky
Not to have a child like that, a daily, inexact puzzle
To solve, with huge teeth and huger gaps between,
And a huge slash of a mouth, and crossed eyes so she looks
Like an angry, laughing grizzly bear on the prowl,
Asthmatic, drooling, sucking at the air around her,
Biting at it sometimes, until finally she can hold it in no longer.
She points to the birds, and my son is calling "help! help!"
As if I couldn't all along have seen or heard.

THE BIG DIFFERENCE

It all comes down to this, all eyes upon it everywhere he goes:
The pizzle, Mr. Peenie-weenie, thing of many names
He hasn't plumbed the thousand-fold
Functions of yet. Not even the toes, when first discovered,
Were so various in their knobby repetitions.
Mother doesn't have one. . . *she's hiding it*, he says. . .
And then insists. . . then moves it forward like a torpedo
Through the water, trying to keep up with it himself.
Already it's an obsession, more important than its uses,
Without which nothing in his daily rounds would have meaning
As he waddles through the world like a bowlegged cowboy
With a brand-new rope, stretching it, stroking it,
Telling it stories, dragging it back and forth
As though it had an agenda of its own, not to be reasoned with,
Something of a burden lately like a baby brother.
His mother smiles and tries to yank his diaper up.
Surprise! such a little thing can become such a big event
In the supermarket, as we hurry down the aisle to catch him,
Giggling, all of us, the men nodding,
The women with their full carts stopped in amusement,
Him guessing what the fuss is all about, watching it subside.

AUTHORITY

When my son would not go potty, *I'm busy*,
Without glancing up from the ranks of toy warriors,
I asked again, louder, beside myself, and he turned toward me
As my own father, with all the authority
Of age and blood, *I said no*, with such clear enunciation
He might well *be* the father, miniaturized man
On horseback with a bland, refusing smile.
Well, here we go again but I'm in charge this time, pal.
I yanked him up and sat him on the stool. *Shit!*
I said into the defiant eyes of our ancestors.
Anywhere a man over his dog yells, *Sit!*,
The dog, who'd rather run, sits.
When I said shit, and he did shit, and smiled
Through his tears and hugged me from the potty,
I knew I had a job at last for which I was cut out.

Porch Life

The old men and the young men, shirtless down the street
On the porch of the two-story tenement,
Drink Coors from cans and pee as they require
In the dirt between the sidewalk and the street.
They call *hello* as I walk by with my toddler son
Who says *how ah ya* like a future member. Sometimes
They call me *sir* as though they don't
Quite remember me, or as though to a boss,
A man to be reckoned with on a job
When they have a job. The group gets larger
As the weather gets warmer. Shirtless,
Shining in the evening heat, they roar
And stagger in circles on the sidewalk.
Snatches of their conversation drift
Into my open window as I try to sleep.
They get the facts mostly loud, the past
In tones of losing and regret.
Nothing changes but an occasional body.
They get their checks on Fridays. The eldest
Grows daisies. The youngest is quietest.

Pilgrims

I meet him in a diner near Seattle,
A man from Florida.
Tucson, I tell him as we chew
The terrible food, talking
So as not to taste. *New York*,
He says, confident, one stranger to another.
Me? *Holyoke, Mass.*, I say, digging
Into my mashed potatoes, buttering
My soft roll shaped like a torpedo,
Wondering why we even stopped
At this place except my son was whining
In his carseat and it was almost noon.

The man from Florida shifts his bulk
And raises one eyebrow as if
About to test some eternal verity:
I knew a guy from Holyoke.
In the Army, in the war.
And I am leaning forward, getting
A sudden rush of photographs that begins
With my old yard and spreads
As if from above, in a helicopter:
The triple deckers, the open porches,
The fathers in the early morning
Swinging their black lunch boxes
Down the narrow walks: *click, click.*

Then, in that sly way older people have
Of pulling rank, he says
You wouldn't know the guy,
I'm old enough to be your uncle,
And winks, until at last
He gives it up: *Jack Sullivan.*
I wipe my son's face and fuss
With his filthy shirtfront
So as not to appear overly eager
Which is a way not to be
On the road in America.

                    I knew the guy,
He was my neighbor. A policeman.
Uh-uh, says the man from Florida
This Jack was a gym instructor,
And then the feeling goes away
Of being somewhere, of being anywhere
As I nibble at the fried chicken
And the walls recede and I begin to lose
The smiling wide and handsome face
Of *my* Jack Sullivan, the yellow house
Eroding at the edges, his mother
In silver braids, his sisters
Rosalie, Sheila, Mary,
And the other whose name I never knew.

The other sister was a Sister, he says.
Yes! Yes! That's my Jack Sullivan!
And I'm almost crying with the victory
And the effort to keep the picture whole,
To take my wife and son and place them
In that house just after World War II
Beside the Sullivan clan, good people
Every one. But the man is not convinced.
He wipes his plate with a slice of buttered bread.

THE BRIDGE OF SIGHS

Believe me when I tell you I have tried
To understand pleasure, the beginning of pleasure,
How I watched my mother

That morning lounging in the red plush chair
In the gray, submerging shadows of the parlor
As she talked on the phone, how I stared

With each of my five years at the tender
Curve of her ankle as it moved down the high instep
Of her dry, clean, pale and perfect foot and over

The toes, underneath to the arch. Oh, it just leapt!
More delicate than the arches of the bridges
Of Venice, built by those gentlemen, the *Doges*,

Paved by the feet of centuries of lovers
And saved from destruction by the American soldiers
On a similar morning

As I watched my mother's foot tense and relax,
And when she smiled down her long body at me,
And stroked my hair, and offered me the smooth beauty

Of her foot, and asked me, yes, to *rub it* just a little,
She said, right into the phone to whomever,
"Ahhh," the *ah* of the beginning of pleasure

That demands, even as it gives itself up,
That leaves you always ready to begin,
Always on the lip of things

Like a young woman standing by the Bridge of Sighs
Waving goodbye to the soldiers of the losing side,
Waving hello to the soldiers of the winning side.

II
SHORT STORY

The Short Story

There was blood and a knife, says the woman.
         One man, or two? No no no, it was dark,
Says the woman, having told this story

         Over and over and it's never the right story
Or the same. Her body is already smaller
         In the story she tells herself. The policeman

Tells the story to a reporter, who tells
         A similar story, but shorter; and in bed
To his lover who tells him yet another,

         Even shorter: *no knife; one man.*
That night he wanders the dark house telling
         The dark the stories. Amazing

How much shorter they've become, how like figures
         In a child's book of monsters
(Where knives are made of paper, and blood

         Is catsup from a bottle), not like stories
Told in an office to a stranger, but smaller,
         Like silver dollars to be held while they remember.

The Early Poetry

This morning on a daybed several blocks from here
A woman you will someday love is being conceived

And you lean to hear the moans, the rhythmic bouncing,
Slightly embarrassed as you squint at the tired faces

Of the salesman and his wife—both immigrants,
Both uncomfortable, he on his lunch break, she out of work.

And no matter how quickly you rush to protect
The baby, the little girl, the young woman, your future wife,

She falls down, she gets a forever black scar
On her knee, she faints on the subway,

A bum thrusts his head up her skirt, and so on,
While you watch and wait, like a movie

Beginning in summer and ending in spring,
With its brief interludes, various dogs, children,

Moments of pensive regret, until you suddenly remember
That you are an 18-year-old clerk

In a white shirt at your clerical pace
With a fading and useless history and hardly

A present tense, and you are seized with impatience
For the future you've glimpsed, so you write it down

In rhymed couplets: *the red car. . . the intruder. . .
The needle. . . the phone call. . . the print of Durer's*

On the yellow wall. . . . You tap your pencil once,
Twice, three times on the metal desk. Now when you wait

You wait with dignity for a future enclosed with rhyme.
As it takes shape, you are inside, observing, inventing.

CARMEN

This is the scene in the factory with the women,
The older women who aren't burning anymore
But slowly burning out, even in repose,
And the young women luscious and giggling
At the long tables in their work clothes. This is Spain,
And not the opera but the movie in which two women
Love one man. The first is dignified and steady
And aging and the other is Carmen.
In such a world the question might be this: Which is
The stronger force, love or passion? And who decides?
In the movie it's supposed to build slowly
And stay hot, the director says, and in response
The older women moan out little untranslatable
Complaints, and the young women, who don't know
Any better, slap the dusty floor with their feet,
Then start the dry, sulphurous clicking
Of flamenco castanets. The dance begins:
Carmen will fight Christina to the death. The knife,
Hidden along a hip, will slash Christina's throat.
All the women know that now by heart.
It is so in the opera, in the play by Mérimée,
It is happening in the story behind the scenes
That echoes the film's story. It is directed
By a man who is himself the lover in question.
In real life the fight would have been ugly
But inconclusive. Probably they would have

Just stood up during lunch break and cursed.
What would you do, and whose story are you living?
The dancer dabbing at her throat in the mirror,
Slowly changing in the changing light, or the dancer
Kept young and available by the gods in perpetual
Punishment? Or are you searching the story's one weakness
That would loose both women in quick stabs upon the world?

BUDDIES

If you saw us talking in the crowded bar, knees touching,
Leaning to whisper, you'd probably think *lovers*, but no,
She likes women. She's talking along like my best buddy

With great delight, some decorum, and as our conversation
Escalates with the Scotch, I get incredibly curious,
And ask for more, to imagine one female body against another.

"The plump one," she says, "and the one with the shoe,"
And then it all goes blank. "Now tell *me*," she says, "it's only fair,"
And despite myself I'm confiding, whispering the good parts,

She's laughing, I'm taking in her hair, her perfume
Which doesn't end but flowers in a touching muskiness.
My whispers draw her closer. Her blouse flutters

In the bar's smoky chatter. She holds her breath
So I can see into the narrow width that represents
Our differences. She rears her head back and she roars.

RED LEAVES

She feels sorry for the courtesans, she said,
And the prostitutes, and the concubines, and the millions

Of wives she holds in contempt for doing
What they had to on pain of death for the men

She hates. She hates the Chinese especially
For raising subservience to such an art: the little girls

Confined to quarters, and the garden,
To marriage, behind curtains, she said. She loves

The poetry they wrote in secret, smuggled out
In brittle paper boats: *Red leaf, I order you —*

Go find someone in the world of men. She hates me,
Too, for being here, a man, though these were eons

At issue, she knew it, and unspeakable
Complexities of culture, and long lines of the dead

Which she stood up against the living lies
Until she could almost climb into their skins,

She said (or something like this), into the small mouths
As they touched a man's wide, crueler, soldier's mouth.

She stood up, crying. She stood in a long line,
Looking back. The woman behind her

Whispered in her ear. She whispered to the long line
Stretched before her. What did you say,

I said before our lives were changed
Without a word of love or sense from either side.

Shame

I must have called him *queer* or said it
To someone who knew him and it got around
Because his mother forbade my company.
I couldn't have meant it as we mean it now
But rather *weirdo, nerd, oddball, dork,*
Which was bad enough and which he was,

I thought, in the 7th grade sense—though even
As my mother spoke in low admonishing tones
Across the living room from the telephone call
And I denied the accusation vehemently
And for days afterwards, I understood
What pain it caused the boy, how such remarks

Enter the bone, settle in, become another
Circle in a person's character, and felt
Ashamed, and never did see him again.
That was 30 years ago. *Never again*
Is punishment enough for an adolescent
Though I have heard he is

A happy family man, a famous sociologist,
Someone I would like to talk with now.
Usually I will be sitting among people
And it will strike me, the slight
Wrenching in the gut, the brief argument
With my younger self—*I didn't mean it*

Quite like that—then the urge
To track him down, to phone him, to explain,
Apologize, analyze like sensible adults.
Then I will have to rise and walk off
As though I were the one cast out, wrapped
In a strangeness I'd tried to give away.

Alternate Lives

Da Vinci, she said, reading
      From her book, has the swallow
Serve for inconstancy —

      Always in motion, unable to endure
The slightest discomfort. Have you ever,
      She asked, cheated on me?

Once? How many times?
      (Leave them alone,
Hours in a borrowed room

      Where the light is weak,
Searching another's body for an answer.
      Wouldn't it be worse

To stay awake all night imagining
      How it would feel to live alone
Sitting like a bachelor or a spinster

      In a straight-backed chair
In a bathrobe sipping whiskey, smoking
      One cigarette after another,

All by yourself watching
    The lilac light arrive—
First swallow arcing over the river—

    And no one to tell
Or have to tell?) Put the book
    Away, he said, and come here.

THE OTHER WOMAN

He removed the photo album from its hiding place
    And showed it to his wife, spread it on the table
Between them and slowly riffled the pages
    And changed the subtle courses of their lives.
They were black and white photos of a woman
    Of the 1940's in a silky looking flowered dress;

The woman wearing his hat, cutting up
    In the lobby of a small hotel; the woman nude,
On a beach, posing with an awkward dignity.
    His wife began to ask the questions,
First general, then specifics,
    The dates (which he remembered), how he met the other
        woman,

How they did it, had he preferred it that way,
    And so it went through the evening into night,
The ancient histories, as he rose to mix the drinks
    And later to refresh the ice, and she
To bank the logs in the fireplace, and they grew wiser
    And more animated beside the glowing coals.

The Older Woman

Blurring at the edges of her hips,
    She rose from the barstool, took my hand,
Leading us down 12th Street, up the elevator
    To her bed. And because of the sad,

Pleasurable aching of one stranger with another,
    I wish I could have said
I'd never seen a more beautiful sight
    When she rose naked from the bed

And put *Swan Lake* on the record player
    To dance the *pas de deux* alone in her swan's
Body with her socks still on and her watch,
    Black swan, white swan, back and forth

Across the half-lit room.
    I didn't take my bow and arrow.
I didn't shoot her by mistake. I didn't love her.
    I was young and we didn't know each other,

So probably we tried to talk
    After the record stopped, by now more mutually
Estranged and desperate than before,
    And I moved closer, and we tried not to sleep.

BLAME

I deserved it, every word, blame
And castigation, the horribly precise words
Knifing out of her mouth as we sat
On a curb one late summer evening on Broadway.

She had a cold and blew her nose incessantly,
Carefully, lady-like,
From a box of tissues in her lap,
Then she'd ball them up and stuff them

Down the grating of a sewer. It was almost
(Though of course it wasn't) impersonal,
Her mouth moving steadily, as if to push
Silence out of the way, one hand

Patting her nose, and me listening,
Blank-faced, consuming, not speaking,
She repeating as if teaching a dog
The simplest restraint, I with no answers,

Nothing to say but sorry, nothing to do
But bear it, and almost (excuse me)
Enjoying it, and she, too, I think,
A cool Manhattan evening,

People walking briskly by at the edge
Of autumn where love loses the sharpness
Of its light, letting the righteous blame
Beam onto me its lasting attention.

A House

for G.

Their mouths blur like leaves caught
    In a crosswind. Lips barely, softly
Touching there, and behind the lips the hard

    White teeth, and further in, pink membranes
Pulsing to seize a breath. How deep is a mouth?
    How far in before you find the other?

Some nights they fall asleep like that.
    Then wake, walk out to check the weather,
Breakfast together, and off to the world

    For a day. All morning and all afternoon
Inside the house shadows change places
    With light. Noon, then twilight, dusk,

Until the shadows become one darkness.
    How thoughtless it looks to a passerby—
Room by room the lamps go on

    As though to repair the harm
The hours have done. But what can you say
    In dark or light that hasn't been said?

Good morning, good night, a kiss again?
        Then, in the body's deepest place—as in a room
Revisited after years away, some space

        You thought of as your own, same radio, same bed
And sink, same view—you meet another
        Passing through, a pilgrim, not quite

Familiar, not quite a stranger. What
        Will you say? *This is where things change,*
Sometimes. This is how some people love.

PARADISE

When the bird saw how innocent they were
    It flew toward the garden
In a swallow's perfect curves.
    So luminous, the woman placed it
In her companion's mouth. They kissed,

    They passed the light between them.
They spoke, and the bird flew out. . . .
    This is the story I tell myself
When I'm most unsure. When I stare
    Out a window at dusk and can't decide:

At times love and at times hate
    Like a phone ringing all night;
Sometimes the truth, sometimes the lie,
    The heart's reasons or the mind's.
Above my room the swallow fascinates

    Even when I feel most sure.
Oh, *come back*, they must have cried,
    Mouths held open in a perfect
Human singing O, the certainties
    Dissolving on their tongues.

How large the sky looks now,
    The swallow's locomotion and obstacle.
Air holds him, makes him graceful,
    Sometimes baffled, a shifting
Helpless light above the garden.

Life Drawing

At night, in the Museum Art School, the men
And women whose daily jobs don't require
Their hands or eyes to surrender to such intimacy,

And the instructor passing over us, and everything
Around the room in shadow gathers to intensify
Light on the model's body, a stranger's, a woman.

The charcoal starts erratically, almost
Of its own accord, though we're hardly aware
Of time anymore, hands moving to match

Body part to body whole, nipple to breast,
The long waist to the shadowy haunch
Like a blue whale rising, falling back

Into the feeding dark. Her eyes are closed.
What could she be thinking of? Her boundaries
Shift between each taken breath. More sure

Of their universe than we, the Old Masters
Drew her as an angel descended, walking across
A country road lost not in thought but motion.

◆

Sundays, the men who hang out at the park
Love to describe women. The young men
Sweep the air with huge motions, like liars

After hours of no bass at the County Reservoir,
With a wink to the boy who caught the fish
But doesn't know yet a woman's figure

Matters enough to tell lies. The old men's hands
Seem to stutter. They might be shaping
The lost map of Thrace—stone house, stone wall,

A horse nibbling grass, clouds from the long neigh.
Hands that labored in stone or wood or dirt
For years, when they're about to fly off the wrists,

Vanish into their pockets.

♦

                    All the postures
Of flesh blur in the overhead lights. The model
Stretches. She puts on her glasses and pads naked

And noisily among us, like a silvery carp
Stranded on a beach, or water, as it overflows
Its banks, seeking a new shape. She wants to see

Just how we have depicted her. Then bends
To pick up her clothes, and with her back to us
Puts them on slowly, bra, panties, and a shirt,

Blue jeans, rubber thongs. What lay there
In a stillness older than statues of gods
Made from clay and spit, is a teenager

In a Rolling Stones T-shirt.

◆

                              If she could have watched
The lumps of charcoal careful to reproduce,
She might have thought: *child playing dead*

At sunset after supper on the front lawn
Under the privet; horizon, hill; hill after hill
Someone cares enough about to sit and draw.

We all love to look. As we can't always touch,
We walk home to more familiar shapes:
The curves follow the light

From the open door, and even as I sit on the bed
And stare, and wake my wife, even as my breathing
Starts to echo hers, there is something I can't have.

The drowsy neck, the hollow back of the knees,
The ear that goes around, the feet
Like a slum at dusk. There is also the body

As a version of habit, skin-deep; body going deeper,
Pleasuring itself even as it pleasures us;
Body the hotel of the spirit, elusive

And presiding, belonging to nothing and to no one.

III
ELEGY

Acts of Will

for Jon & Barbara Anderson

On certain nights the bad mood takes you
    By surprise, and all the faces you meet
Shrink to the bleakest, farthest stars. Oh
    Take a bus as far as it goes
To the city's edge. That no man's land
    Where it idles, breathing like a house alone

In an empty field. You don't, of course,
    And the night shoves you along
In unhooked trains of association — old regrets,
    Blunders, humiliations, loves, the dead —
And nothing stops you until the end
    Defeats the mind's self-repairing chemistry.

What draws us into such a narrow place,
    A nameless, causeless, heartless chasm?
Doubts we thought we'd overcome?
    Our body's occasional need for despair?
Or is it the numb bliss, oblivion,
    We desire? Wouldn't it be better

To talk to ourselves in a dark
    Of our own choosing, go home,
Phone a pal or read a book, dance to the radio's
    Late ballast of music? How long you
Stand there, fascinated. You touch your cheek,
    You need a shave. What casual truths

Such moments absorb, those small decisions
    Arrived at in the dark. Stall
A moment longer. Then whistle,
    Sing, grin, my friend. Welcome
To the loneliest communion, an act of will
    From which you won't return quite whole.

CONVERSATION WITH THE DEAD
Carol Marcus 1946-1969

It was a minor argument with my future sister-in-law
on the way to the wedding. When we arrived for the
ceremony, I apologized, and the more specifically I
explained where I'd been wrong, the more intransigent
she became, leaning against the altar, refusing my
meager *mea culpa*. The whole incident got smaller, and
never went away.

She died some months later. Now when I rehearse my
explanations to the dead, hers come first. We are
all dressed up, as at the wedding. We sit across
from each other, and raise our hands, as if in
surrender, or as if to play a child's game, knowing
that the winner wins and the loser, well, the loser
always wants to play again. I am at my most reasonable,
most contrite, and still I can't stop explaining.

Familiar

In Memoriam Egon Marcus 1910-1982

This is the shape of a man in sleep, breathing,
    Not breathing, a moth between shadow and light,
Between wife and daughter, and the rain they watch
    Out the window for hours, water, air,
Then nothing, bright miscellaneous debris.

    Asks an uncle, "Ach, *was ist ein Mann?*"
The question flutters from cousin to cousin.
    The black umbrellas open. Someone tosses
A handful of dirt, and what has been given

    Returns to earth. The widow asks, "*What is a widow?*"
And smiles over the melon, the fish, the bread,
    The coffee, the candle that burns yellow
All night for a week, while in other rooms

    Things shatter, a vase, then a mirror,
Accustomed to a different touch, as though
    Through a new house finding each thing
Unfamiliar, belonging, familiar yet wrong,
    The soul, breathed out, now runs amok.

Religious Feeling

When the son challenged his father to arm-wrestle
At the kitchen table and the father allowed

The challenge to persist without acknowledgment,
Spreading like an after-dinner stain,

The atmosphere got larger, the room surrounding them
Became like the air released from a church organ booming

Suddenly into the shuffling, unrepentant silences.
The mother held their clamped hands

In her light grip, and glanced out the window
At a woman raking and a man bending to retrieve

A toddler from a pile of leaves. How calm and strong
Her own husband seemed, balanced on a wooden chair,

Knowing age would erase this scene like a slow
And steady wave across a beach. And her son,

If only he had the sense yet to count
The taken breaths between the challenge and the act. . . .

She began to count *One two three*
Holding her glance out the window

At the child still burrowing in the maze of light
And dark the wind prepared itself to take away.

ACTS OF GOD

I wonder where he's headed, what drives him
To pace the several miles of boulevard
Every afternoon, less like a bum
Than a holy man on a holy errand.
His great dwarf's head collapses downward
To read the unrolling cuneiform of sidewalk. (He wears
A dark, emphatic, ghetto European sort of hat.)
And, look, he is pausing, stopping now,
Beside the Hopi woman handing out
Jehovah's Witness tracts. She stands there
With a look of bland fatigue.
Now they are chatting, giggling actually.
Both are tiny, driven, elderly, and if not wise
Then full of themselves this afternoon,
As though having waited all their lives
For this moment to stop him, and then to shake her loose.

ACROBATICS

for Gibb Windahl

First comes disbelief. Then double-take.
Then he begs, whines, tells a joke
I can't hear but see the expectations
Of laughter in the way he cocks
His head, the thin black man,
The charmer, weaving while he talks
The way a person rocks imperceptibly
When given an infant to hold.

All the while the overweight
Young saleswoman behind the counter
In the liquor store is saying, "No,"
In a monotone, knowing
She'll have to repeat it endlessly,
"You're drunk," and smiles
What seems a compassionate smile
As the man slowly kneels

And stiffens his arms and leans
Upon them the entire weight
Of 40 years or so, the creases
In his face, his shining optimism,
And does the handstand, legs
Together, barely quivering,
And in a deep bass sings,
Ratta tatta cumbalacha ala whazoo. . . .

The store begins to fill
With customers. The woman
Turns to their needs. The man
Removes a bottle of Fleischman's
In full sight of everyone
And steps outside for a long, good night.
As I pass him on the street, he smiles,
Says, *She hurt me so sweet.*

CELEBRITY

Tony Bennett

He shines through the airport like a retreating star.
Through lounge after lounge he is a slowly
Disappearing glow as our faces rise.
Nodding, we raise our voices, we wave.
It's like one of those "waves" at a football game,
All the bodies part of the rhythm
Of what we missed and had not known
We missed, and finally we belong; and he, too,
In his way, with his deep, immutable tan,
And hair hardly a shade too dark, walking
Somehow too slowly, like an aging ex-champ
Who enters the ring and shadowboxes for the crowd,
Dressed in a dark blue suit that shows
Just how large and powerful he really is,
Larger than any of us, for we are finding ourselves
Particularly small today, quite ordinary, on the verge
Of panic actually, fearful of the very sky.

Yard Cats

for Nancy Pitt

I never see them born
    But they arrive in early spring
Almost fully formed,
    Toddling out from under
A pile of logs or a porch,
    This season's first litter,
Two white, one orange.
    The orange mother cat
Sends out her electric
    Ruff of fur, hissing to protect.
Later, I'll feed them
    Because they are
The yard's requirements,
    But I won't tend them
Like a garden in
    And out of season,
And I won't name them
    Anything but colors.
When they disappear
    I know they'll be replaced.
They aren't particular
    In memory like events
But continuous like seconds
    In the hours at dusk.
Rising from the shade
    They turn beneath my idle hand.

ACTS OF GRACE

All one summer I thought about God.
This in the factories, and at an age
When I'd just as soon have felt
Like any ordinary apprentice machinist,
A recently graduated high-school kid no different
From anyone else. All around us
The din of huge machines, routers and lathes
That cast the high windows with metal dust,
And now and then the random lap of waves
Off a nearby canal creating a timeless,
Sanctuary baffle. I'd let my mind work
Until the thought broke
When the whistle blew. One time one of the men
Must have sensed the burden of my thought
Because he asked a question so generalized
It felt intimate. I don't remember what
But I must have been amazed,
As I am now by any unexpected, heartfelt,
Endlessly answerable question.
Maybe I felt that slurring in the brain
That happens a split second into an accident.
Anyway, I didn't so much decide to quit
As I drifted into other jobs, college, and so on.

I thought about it just a while ago. Probably
I was so shy back then God kept me company.

Or God was pure attention, abstract, like a mantra.
It hardly matters now. It so happens
The poplars are in leaf. Bordering each yard
The white perennial African daisies, and poppies
Whose languid, yellow petals seem to palpitate,
Like flesh. I was out walking.
I glanced up. On a balcony above the avenue
Stood a very old woman dressed in a robe
And slippers. I saw that in the raised circle
Of her arms she held a photo in a frame.
Then she was moving, she was dancing with the photo,
A waltz, as though she'd heard the call
While ironing and it just fell on her
Like old clothes, or spring snow. And just as suddenly
As she began she stopped and bent her body
Out a little over the neighboring yards,
Rows of houses, trees, flowers in their beds.
Sometimes this world's the safest place to be.

At the Indoor Shopping Mall

for Tony Hoagland

Either the snow's persistence or inertia sat me down,
After I'd run my errands, beside a blue-tiled fountain,

And wherever I looked young couples wheeled
Their sleeping infants, and in and out of shops

Went wives with trailing identical husbands
In brightly-colored trousers. "Isn't it lovely?"

Said an elderly woman beside me on the bench
Beside the circular fountain. Her dress

Was a field of flowers. Over the flowers the spray
From the water was blue as the waters of a bottomless

Lagoon, and I there beside them, emptied of need
And happy at last—until I saw, way down below,

What seemed the movement of a fish, lantern-jawed
And glowering, eyeless as a rock, and the slow

Muffling weight of water burying itself
In water, breathing it in, and further down

Like a vast and stupid secret, the plain bottom
We can never see but know. "Isn't it getting late?"

She said. She rose from the bench, a field
Of endlessly intricate wild-flowering weeds,

Then came the soft and airy *whoosh* of revolving doors
And shoppers coming through with armfuls of packages

And it was December again in the north
In the windowless light of perpetual waters.

Born in 1942 in Holyoke, Massachusetts, Steve Orlen was educated at the University of Massachusetts and the University of Iowa, where he graduated from the Writers Workshop. His previous full-length poetry books include *Permission to Speak* and *A Place at the Table*. He has won grants from the National Endowment for the Arts, the Arizona Commission on the Arts, and the Fondation Karolyi, as well as the George Dillon Memorial Award from *Poetry* Magazine. His poems have appeared in such places as *American Poetry Review*, *Anateus*, and *The Atlantic Monthly*. He is Director of the creative writing program at the University of Arizona.